THE HUNGER

Also by D.C. Reid

THE HUNGER

D.C. REID

Ekstasis  Editions

National Library of Canada Cataloguing in Publication Data

Reid, D. C. (Dennis C.)
    The hunger / D.C. Reid.

ISBN 1-894800-31-1

    I.†Title.

PS8585.E4486H85 2004   C811'.54   C2004-907060-3

Published in 2004 by:
Ekstasis Editions Canada Ltd.   Ekstasis Editions
Box 8474, Main Postal Outlet   Box 571
Victoria, B.C. V8W 3S1   Banff, Alberta T0L 0C0

THE CANADA COUNCIL | LE CONSEIL DES ARTS   BRITISH
FOR THE ARTS | DU CANADA   COLUMBIA
SINCE 1957 | DEPUIS 1957   ARTS COUNCIL
                                    Supported by the Province of British Columbia

The Hunger has been published with the assistance of grants from the
Canada Council and the Cultural Services Branch of British
Columbia.

For Deborah Nilsen

—*my gift is my words and these ones are for you*

…once you have the solution to the conundrum there can be no more speculation, no more discussion. The subject is dead.

Anne Szumigalski

…the moon is a woman and the woman gives birth to herself over and over.

Gail Anderson-Dargatz

TABLE OF CONTENTS

The Hunger

Then The Further Day 13
Leaning Off The Transom Scraping A Twisted Skeg 14
In The Time It Takes The Shark To Come 16
Eagles 18
The Day Diana Died 20
The Hunger 22
My Father Was A Coward. He Shot Himself Without Necessity. 24
The Willingness To Receive Without Resistance 26
The Mackerel And I A Man 28
A Microphone Is Only As Good As The Speaker 30

Simple Things

Simple Things 35
The Ache That May Also Be A Candle 37
Outside This Door 38
I am thinking about a beautiful almond in the brain 39
It's All Coming Back To Me Now 41
The Day We Will All Be Dead 42
The Irrational Belts Of Love 44

I Shall Fear No Evil

I Shall Fear No Evil In The Valley Of The Nitinat 47
If you don't know what you're thinking, you're not anywhere. 48
Hakai Pass 50
The Visitation of Hakai And 51
Hakai Pass Revisited 53
The Needley Teeth Of Salmon Fill My Hands
        With Yellow Liquid 55

For Deborah Wherever You May Find Her

Perhaps The First Love Poem   59
Comes A Soft Soft Inside Me I Never Meant To Offer Up While
    Taking A Bite Of Thigh Or Breast Or Sway Of Back   61
Any Declaration No Matter How Tentative Is A Trip To
    Somewhere Else   62
Sheepdog Trials Metchosin Sunday   64
For Women Who Graze The Melting Far   66
Think Of Life As Severing Connections Until There's Nothing
    Left To Hold Us   68
Deb At Crossroads 46:   70
Deborah The Director Who Stops The Violence
    Against Women   72
Alone Again With The Scent Of You On My Hands   74
For Deborah Wherever You May Find Her   76

The Earth For Gestures Words Are Not Enough

Elegy From A Slumber I Can't Retrieve   79
Carmanah or the nature of[1]   81
Why we enter each other's lives and how we fit together is more
    than is given us to know. And yet that's what we want,
    isn't it? That's what we want to understand.
  In the beginning of me is the beginning of everything   84
  Youth a kind of ample green flower   86
  This close a flung arm is a gesture futile and grand   87
  How completely we are forced at the mercy of reliving   89
  Of fierce September here briefly by the foghorn on the point 90
  Now and finally the festive amygdala   91

Acknowledgements   93

THE HUNGER

THEN THE FURTHER DAY

She saw the queen of heaven once and kept the vision in her soul
No one believed what she had seen, no one believed what she heard.
                    Leonard Cohen

Myth is history we need.
                    Jan Zwicky

As if the white wasps in their paper casings
                              were symbols of wisdom
and so a promise I could trust.

As if the rain falling fitfully on the house-rounded shore
                              were a selflessness and giving in
to destiny were admirable completely.

As if the land was not to be heard at night pouring winter through
itself to Gonzales Bay.

Mornings of white light, my paler self walks the water untethered.

And even before me, Spanish captains with black between their teeth,
squiring names – San Juan, Esperanza, Escalante. They could not
escape through the residue of memory.

In its time, when it is ready, the ocean turns and sings the calcium
from bone until it is no more.

Come on let me hold you, won't you let me hold you, like
Bernadette would do.

LEANING OFF THE TRANSOM SCRAPING
A TWISTED SKEG

If God were the uncertain would you cling to him?
Paul Valery

*Basho said: avoid adjectives of scale, you will love the world
more and desire it less.*
Robert Hass

One could just lean into a green horizon

                       the Upanishads predict is
the end of all mankind:

      desire, all we are. And so I lay hands on my head
                     and pour in that
pureness we have agreed to agree comes only from the heart.

Forget the house the bank uses to chain me to my future, the com-
promise of children, health.

The sea again, like the loose-limbed abandon of sleep.

Invisibly and without consent, layers of epidermis pinken their way to glory and drift away 200,000 times a day.

There and there,
                acres of dock laid out like linen in the bleaching fields.
The strain of clevis and u-bolt thick as my thumb.

Numb to my armpits and reaching the green halo behind my shadow.

Way out there at the ends of my arms, barnacles slice my fingers.

Red plumes rise from my hands.

As I was saying, the simplicity of April. Trillium in the waste land.
A pool of clothes upon the dock.

IN THE TIME IT TAKES THE SHARK TO COME

The way a worm will reach out innocent of the suffering it brings to a meal.

I might order a creamy bolonnaise, tender breast of marlin marinated brown.

I flip pennies for the April-noon pleasure of watching copper thoughts of some not-too-intelligent Einstein trickle their way to theorem.

Maybe, as the psychoanalysts opine through half-moon glasses, all art is a failure to resolve neuroses.

Maybe. Maybe the sun is a sister taken for granted or a familiar brontosaurus lifting its leafy meal from islands east where black-gummed Spaniards languished for Vitamin C.

I propose upon my lofty terrace with its chairs propped together like used people, that gravity is cumulative, its need for the old is greater; Queen E. zigs and zags her way to oblivion.

In its passing and in its leaving the sea is strands of hair past the

Turkey Head. Reveals it then the bones beneath what we take to be the truth of things:

the seal with its prehensile whiskers prefers the ripped-out gills of salmon.

Comes the beautiful predator with the burning green eyes, snouting blood like some weird aphrodisiac, the seal from which it can scalpel a grapefruit of flesh.

Then their turning together while sea lice cinch my arms like bolo ties. Just like that, kindred assassins in the morning, women in gauze of red.

This cold blooded kingdom of smell that all but man can enter.

Like the end of a movie a seagull risen from its lacustrane world one-legged on the cafe railing chokes to death politely on a starfish, some slow-witted human emerging from its pod.

EAGLES

elegy for Charles Lillard

Their hanging in midair is not a reprieve, only a phase of the inevitable.

Similarly, my hands hang pendulous, as though they died some days previously, bleed quietly into my jeans.

I think of Charles who is not here, the way we do and don't tell children of Santa.

I think of Charles with daylight in his eyes, of the cancer in his spine.

The gender politicians are wrong: the sea is a man. It is not without sensitivity or muscle,

the coho slithering the boat, hook in the pad of my thumb. My eyes rise the wall of wave coming down my shoulder

all the way from Indonesia to make the present known to me, the glittering skin of glass reptiles, glass horses, naked as rooms of chandeliers.

I think of his face in decline: waxen, yellow; the way krill have no other fate than to offer themselves colourless in the breath of whales.

The day I fished with a shoeful of blood and spent the night removing the knife from my foot.

Look at the beginning of darkness in the lips when we tell a child the truth about this brief gift of being alive.

They gather on the northern shore among the brooding moons, scenting the weary land. The windmill sings the acrid flame of broom upon the hill.

Only September and pale-headed eagles turn the world this way and that, as if to rise from all this bruisedness, and fall 30 miles toward the broken mountains of America. Those that don't achieve the dream succumb to freedom. It gives first food, then death, the only word that could kill them:

sea,

this masculine frightening I go out on and go out on.

THE DAY DIANA DIED

To reinvent from across the room that we have purchased for now in my underpants my own way to write exact as fingerprints having left the bed to smoke and pen a spurt of nothing on a napkin.

In ribs of sun on the other side an island of thigh and wetness render a woman. And before, our bodies together like starfish.

We have faced our death today, the disappeared morning, sixty miles through unseen freighters and duplicity of fog. For us the thin sweat of spiders and blazing hands upon the helm.

The steps we take to freedom are small and matter only to ourselves: the warm bodies with whom we close our eyes.

Lush, half mad the scent of us descends with us from the long sun

for a ritzy sort of dinner, food upon our forks and the news that in our
love a princess died.

The punctured heart jumps on its ribs and you say *this is happening.*

How like foxes the jackals with delicate whiskers curved and lacquered
red. She has her foot beside her ear her white eyes as stars jerk for
her this last time across a blue summer evening.

All right then, responsibility. The poet passes to a faraway country
close by. While my tongue descends on her vein like a blind arm,
while I look in the mirror until my face doesn't make sense anymore,

the sound forks make on china. The sun exploding in a wine glass.
The legs of Cambodian children.

THE HUNGER

Is there a benign mythology of colour that accounts for all this ice?
Take that blue boat in the blue distance where sea and sky become
each other. I am in that boat and I'm not blue.

Our talk, for now I've written two of us, is of the coyote spoon and
its green glow eye, the clover leaf, mint tulip, the hootchie let down.

Seamlessly the sea turns, landscape on a journey to nowhere distinct.
It pulls us through the back of ourselves and the Race in a roundness
at ease with the moon.

Our talk, when it comes again, is of the lost poem, the raven who
flew straight for the curve of the earth, the Pacific, and could not be
reconciled it was a water too far;

of the disease of creativity; the cheery probability one in five of poets
will kill themselves. What gives January the right to make skeletons
of everything?

Graham Green, for instance, burning for roulette. He pulled the trigger
in his ear and quenched a winning with alcohol. Pointless, for desire
is liquid too and falls toward the mind, the hand.

                              To what weakness
does one lean willingly? The white powder rising to the pleasure centre
of the brain is poetry.

And before that rush the other rush when blood worms in the fit saying, "I love you." Why oh why do veiny-eyed cormorants line up like accountants in fatal January?

I wipe my thighs. My hands look out at you, ask the question: what does it take for men to be friends? There is a song in the nerves of things. It is lightning in flesh.

The club I raise and death snaps along their bodies. Corpses in the fish bucket, blood on the legs of our pants.

How islands bathe in the gristling sea, sensual as rounds of winter skin. On the rocks Jurassic, yellow-circled eyes. Cormorants snout the air for death and shiver in all their shabby hunger.

Idling back to Pedder, the boat chooses its path, a horse, reins upon its withers, haunches shifting like women. The harbour rips open like the bones of pregnant animals.

Again there is the flesh-starved heron frozen into the shoreline, the wild pathetic beauty we are all in.

What have I forgotten?   Be at peace, white heart.
Go easy, blood upon your knees.

MY FATHER WAS A COWARD.
HE SHOT HIMSELF WITHOUT NECESSITY.

Ernest Hemingway[1]

...trying to write the poem in one fell swoop and if failing, cast it out forever.

Erin Mouré

...and my poems, the broken ones that will never be seen. These I keep for myself. They are the other silence, the one that sings to me when my friends are gone and the night moves with great slowness in my hands.

Patrick Lane

Sometimes I think I'm gonna lose my mind but i don't think I ever really will.

Woody Guthrie

I have heard Coleridge talking, with eager musical energy, two stricken hours, his face radiant and moist, and communicate no meaning whatsoever...

Thomas Carlyle

I've had eighteen straight whiskeys. I think that's a record.

Dylan Thomas

I would like to hang myself on the nearest branch of the cherry trees standing now in full bloom.

Hugo Wolf

I hadn't washed my hair for three weeks... I hadn't slept for seven nights... I had followed the green luminous course of the second hand, the minute hand and the hour hand of the bedside clock through their circles and semicircles, every night for seven nights, without missing a second or a minute or an hour.

Sylvia Plath

The thought of suicide came to me as naturally then as the thought of improving life had come to me before... And I quit going hunting with a gun, so that I would not be too easily tempted to rid myself of life.

Leo Tolstoy

Do I deserve credit for not having tried suicide – or am I afraid the exotic act will make me blunder,

Lord Byron

Dearest, I feel certain I am going mad again... I can't fight any longer.

Virginia Woolf

---

[1] *The root of the evil lies in the constitution itself, in the fatal weakening of families from generation to generation... the root of the evil certainly lies there. And there's no cure for it.*

Vincent Van Gogh

THE WILLINGNESS TO RECEIVE
WITHOUT RESISTANCE

We're just a habit like saccharin and I'm habitually feeling kind of blue, but each time I try on the thought of leaving you, I stop, stop and think it over.
                    Paul Simon

The U.S. is to blame for the 9/11 patriot attacks.
                    Saddam Hussein

I could say that hands tore the world apart on a day the wind chimes were shouting.

My father fell out of his sky screaming into orange Ploesti corn, fields where Germans jackbooted past his nose, the tree they sawed by hand to land a plane.

Hammer in hand I beat the stucco into submission.

70 years since Hitler's father folded his son in half and half again until he needed to teach the Jews a lesson.

I sledge the plate and cripples, snip the chicken wire free.

The 1898 Salon critic proclaimed, "Never has anyone had the idea of excising a man's brains in this way and smearing them on his face." To him (whose name we no longer remember) I say,

Rodin's Balzac persists, you critical swine, and beauty:

the eagle fir on the cliff leaned into the wind until the rain washed its
roots delicate as alveoli.

The 1873 Douglas fir where eagles will sit no more lured the deck, the
pool in a wayward ribbon down the bank.

I cut man-size chunks from the white-hazy wall to pass a Bobcat,
backhand sweat from my chin.

Oh Hitler, Hitler, if you touched the edge only once and were
irretrievably changed, would you if you knew?

I hate the wind myself, how it wrecks the heads of trees

Happiness is a season without identity. It swells toward the tulips
and leaves us listening.

I might dream this onto you my parents: holding hands in the broken
wall, staunching the rags of February light in sturdy shoes.

There is also Her Majesty's syrup tin, with its lion and bees, honey
taking the place of blood.

THE MACKEREL AND I A MAN

Loneliness makes gods of us all.
George McWhirter

It's terrible… to think that all I've suffered and all the
suffering I've caused might have arisen from the lack of a
little salt in my brain.
Robert Lowell

Van Gogh drowned his canvas with impatience and lost an ear and
then his life waiting for lithium.

The fault wasn't his, nor Woolf or Berryman,
                              Sexton, Pasternak,
Fitzgerald; the taste of gun-blue oil that Hemingway ate – all humans
with too much eye in them.

I a man with thick glasses write poems strewn with body parts.
                              The Somass tumbles to its
maker. "I am me and never me," is a song on the skin when hair
walks on end.

Nosed unknowing from sea to clearer enemy,

                         the mackerel yanks its jaw like a human hit
with a bullet.

What is an estuary but evidence of more desirable destinations?

The river pressed it to its lips and sucked every molecule of itself,
                                        delicate, zebra fish,
jaggering in the shallows.

How I fear this beating heart of mine. How the fungus will eat my
eyes and pull my lips across my teeth. Who could deny me the
choice of fire, the end of August, swollen so with appetite?

Eyes wide open and round, silver ingots sink into paradise.

The elephant-leg willow weeps September and milltown girls
languishing for life to begin.

Here comes I dragging dead sockeye, scraping knuckles up the gangplank.
Red shirt, red face, red fish.

The Somass flows only to the sea and takes its life.
                                  Eternity does not yawn out. Eternity
is not here.

A MICROPHONE IS ONLY AS GOOD
AS THE SPEAKER

...rediscovering our stolen [Canadian] history.
Milton Acorn

7% of Americans believe Elvis is still alive.
Much More Music

*It is inevitable that each of us will be misunderstood; this, it
seems, is part of twentieth-century wisdom.*
Carol Shields

Sa-sa-wat-in said: if not this legend then what?

Narvaez who emphasized the killing with his finger and thumb
touching just so?

This Spaniard, this 1791 Dago, this conquistador who exchanged the
Renaissance for a tin-lipped hat and at whose feet a disgruntled
historian might lay the blame of smallpox.

A stream over rocks yields to stay together and follows purpose it
cannot avoid.

Sarita let's call it in deference to the great Narvaez who found the
broken rock a just altar to march Keeshan savages to bone splinters.

He fell among the waves in his heavier-than-life hat. Banfield in his
gumboots.

Or so someone convinced Alfred Carmichael who convinced
R. Bruce Scott who wrote a book of acid free paper the mildew
spores of which fly into my nostrils like the trillionth second after
the bang.

What was said was this: when the moon was full of Kloquana festival
the Clallam climbed the broken rock and rendezvoused Ohiaht
skulls with stone hammers in the long house where shadows climbed
the wall unsuccessfully.

Shades Butterfield of the roany eyebrows maintains the Spanish
kick-stepped from Execution Rock to God.

If you don't believe me ask chief Louis Nookemus, ask his voice kept
inside the National Museum by Eugene Arema, hear the stamping of
his walking stick at Aguilar point that sunny afternoon.

I want Eleanor Wachtel and the gift of making people speak in
truths.

D.C. Reid will tell her no one knows the names of the four small
heads who swam the phosphorescent sea and fell together to make
an Ohiaht nation from two boys who took their sisters for their
wives.

SIMPLE THINGS

SIMPLE THINGS

Like being someone else:

imagine a man with greying temples pausing with his spatula over
the first element. Water, he thinks and some of it sizzles to salt in
front of his astonishment.

If there were a slow camera to record such a thing, a photograph to
protect all that is unique about this man, the promise of his greasy-
cornered photos, kids smeared through various rites of passage.

"It must be the ocean," he says, longing for his daughter and props
himself against the rose-flowered walls, here and here, as though the
room were soft and padded and would enfold him.

Imagine his daughter sitting down to dinner with its forest above her
kitchen green and lurching as a petrified wave; he knows that
photographs cannot in themselves cause agony:

the Halloween V was the Phantom in her great grampa's fedora, and
S was Tina Turner though no one could tell.

The roses come and go as he wades the rolling kitchen, pokes his
dinner for one.

For all his lorazepam blandness, his "I'm fine, just fine." he cannot
focus on metaphor. The salt

he can taste, that fecund almost rotting air of the sea that pulls with hidden strings. They are the same as those that stream from the 25 photos of his S&V growing older and older.

He tongues white from the corner of his mouth and cannot for the moment rid his mind of iguanas. "Nothing's going on in here," he says though for all he and I know no one else is here or within miles of this little grey house on this woody little block.

There are the usual miracles of course, boiling water for tea from the inside out by vibrating its molecules. "That makes life sort of almost okay."

The man with greying temples in his rosy-walled room puts his hand on the element to see if it'll burn. This failure to trust himself

is a cobra that dips forward and the wee nip hurts only a little but its small deposit, as easily missed as a shot or two of semen, grows into something altogether different.

S&V learned the speed light travels away in the languid green classes in the too long days of September, afternoon lounging gently on their shoulders.

O, for him, the weeping jumps out of me at the most inopportune time.

Here I am with my dead broccoli, my strips of ginger chicken. Touch a napkin to my lips. Imagine I am cleansed.

THE ACHE THAT MAY ALSO BE A CANDLE

The crisis consists precisely in the fact that the old is dying and the new cannot be born; in this interregnum a great variety of morbid symptoms appears.
Antonio Gramsci

Lies may be a tissue but the slightest truth may also be a rope.
Anon

Sometimes the smallest breeze can set me to shivering:

freedom from the old photographs,
Vanessa in belief on Santa's knee on the day her parents died.

Samantha and the importance of being 19, a blue truck and that willingness to put the foot to the floor and pile on distance the way the coastal morning shoves horizons of blue together.

Wrinkles across the forehead of my child bending to the keys that Mozart also knew.

The spare bedroom, the empty bed, the pillow like a grave.

I might claim to know the trees in my yard, the branch rubbed raw by years of rope that swung size 2 heels on a trajectory to Newtonian physics.

Children do not need fathers anymore.
I must hit myself in the head to learn more correctly to believe.

Whisper and blow me away.

OUTSIDE THIS DOOR

Outside this door the lawn, the curve of the shore thrown up
for the eye,

this docile city I might offer my lungs to wake.

Instead one of my hips twisted forward just so, the quadriceps a little
violin.

This day I think into that other time and within that thinking also
the belief this day will not come…
                                        a far light in the stirred-up
morning, like the fear of children.
Real as if my children died, not poetry pain.

I believe myself up the mountain on St. George Terrace where hope
is set sail among the high white houses, the sour taste of a ladybug
signifying spring.

The sun is this moment visible, the bell dong, donging in sea light
under clouds spring wet and red as lips.

How then what I avoid comes after me: Vanessa's high-topped purple
runners, against a bedroom wall of my home, dust…

my tendon, as I said, the bow, the violin of my hip.

To play such riddled music, wake this whole damn city the name of
a dead queen.

This way I run, sixteen miles into middle age, and this I don't believe.

I AM THINKING ABOUT A BEAUTIFUL ALMOND IN THE BRAIN

Erin Mouré

We imagine we are always the first to step across the threshold
of our days – Is that not my shadow by the door? – and take a piece
of bread and break it

just so it opens its white heart proclaiming only we have come of age.
And so, escaping his father's blows, the boy filled his skin with alcohol and vanished from his life.

I found his young body wrapped in himself and the cottonwood in
my own familiar valley distant from the cliff he attempted to fly.

And for me here, ever conscious, narrative technique fails:

the way for me a cloud comes to the mountain and in its passing,
when it is finished with it, the mountain remains, steadily white,
altogether changed and sailing, over February.

Memory. Useless as that hole in men's underpants only boys use.

I was a kid on the edge, the trout a miracle in the empty kingdom beneath my feet.

Simply breathing, gently opening fan-shaped red gills, calling all life. What can be said? The cherry blossom tree does, the seasons turn and we become more and

more like ourselves. We live life flung-out, like a sheet snapped on a bed. Someone flies away from here someone remains. Today the doors close like vaults.

Two otherwise humane men in black leather sling the body in a plastic bag into the helicopter.

Somewhere there is the silent splendour of the shy white brain behind its petals of bone. "Fold them back," something whispers. "Be," they say. "We will all one day, much against our will, build the earth with ourselves."

In the helicopter now helpless as it twitches through cloud beyond the runway. A jumbo rumbles through the roots of my hair. 140 knots with closed eyes into nothing behind nothing but a ripening plexiglass windscreen.

Technique fails; we have contact.

IT'S ALL COMING BACK TO ME NOW

Reading the poem too quickly and I make it into a kind of
meaningless prose.

As if meaning could only cohere to a mind attuned to what is not
first here.

What holds a bird up? Certainly not something invisible,

and in the lawn
the grass bleeding tears again

in the sea fire falling from the sun
the very Japanese barnacle.

Birds get pushed around the sky, an explosion of feathers on the blades
and zero inside, but several layers inside a short digestive tract

the cat.

I hold my hands down, show my palms on my thighs,
a flower saying let it go, stop talking. Be.

THE DAY WE WILL ALL BE DEAD

What point responsibility when no one remains indignant, no
scores are kept?

Just now the sheet lifting cool from my nose in a room too white.

Can we criticize the dead, our mad rush into oblivion,
or say we never came this way?

Is a casket a door or that fiery little bottle into which cadavers are
ladled.

And the oxygen without a soul clinging here, like saran wrap. The
day earth slows down what I invent the sudden lung gaspingness of
air the thin skin in space invisible,

no fireworks. The houses rising into space, the clothesline and colour
coordinated bread makers, the street we walk down going nowhere
in summer you and I and

the domestic sigh

the dizziness of ordinary good fortune.

And the rain wet asphalt bending up, our wings not here. Alligheri,
Picasso, the lighter dirts rising,

or, say, it's 6:00 am all day and the neutrinos have hissed us into
vapour hours ago a kind of round museum this small tectonic
squishy ball this no-light-of-its-own blue-green reflector

an archeological dig for those we know not come to tsk tsk over our
demise

greedily making tenure the day I die we die we all die. The silence of God

(is)

the universe is night on the other side of air.

Lumbar yellow sun through the eastern window a morning corpse,
waxily beautiful if you don't think, you better not.

THE IRRATIONAL BELTS OF LOVE

In my dreams the baby tigers are gentle – they cling to me as
I stroke them, they tender me their warmth.
Lynn Crosbie

It is a way of surviving, you see: freezing within ourselves
things that would otherwise kill us.
Neil Bissoondath

And more, the braced teeth of Vanessa, the combing of oars and too
many crows in the locks.

Durrance Lake where cutthroat bear their delicately spotted flanks
and throats.

The fly line and the hook like an eyelash by her eye and she began to
cry in snow that fell with great arm sweeps of indifference
all around us little wrinkles on the water.

Durrance Lake a winter made of April where otherwise tulips open
lips and I sing I am sorry I am so sorry,
the smallest sugarest whiplash on Vanessa's cheek the hook missiled past.

These memories which in another head could be tormentous. These
be my own I celebrate.

I SHALL FEAR NO EVIL

I SHALL FEAR NO EVIL IN
THE VALLEY OF THE NITINAT

My weariness amazes me, I'm branded on my feet.
Bob Dylan

*Chronic Fatigue Syndrome is a disease for which there is no
known cure.*
DSM III

The mark the chisel carves in marble is a servant of the greater blow.

Where the Nitinat eats the land it tosses the tails and gills, the gentle
fungus in green and yellow and grey.

They have come back the shape of rotten umbrellas, dog salmon,
keta-toothed to hold the does in place and break in the breaking
water.

Carcasses in the green tunnel trees, eyes pecked out and eagles
important in their tonsures like minor deities Ghiberti refused to hit
with a hammer.

Spanish moss grows its pasty flesh across the knubby waders
and the Nitinat is a conversation that falls away from everything it
tells me it is. I am allergic to the blue, blue sky.

Back to my needle. The stainless shank slips among the layers of my leg.
I am the artisan of a tired gargoyle.

Number 29 syringe, cyanocobalamin hangs from my thigh. First a
ladybug climbs down then half a strawberry.

"Things aren't always about who I am," I say to October branches
and suck a thigh until my teeth show.

IF YOU DON'T KNOW WHAT YOU'RE THINKING, YOU'RE NOT ANYWHERE.

A poem is as neural as love;
the rut of rhythm that veers the mind.

Anne Michaels/D.C. Reid

Fine words when I can't conceive.

Fear in the afternoon in the long waves, crust of tear on my eyeballs,
the wind that takes my hat, propeller the shape of Swiss cheese.

Not the tick of the reel, not the spilling water.

Slimed with diamonds. The reel burns a crescent of pain from finger
to wrist. Anus to gill and the slice of the cabbage head.

I smash my hand with the club and the fist needs storing in a pocket.

Freighters pass unseen, cities in the solemn light. So it is safe for them and me the grazing wakes of death.

The sea again, pulling my knuckles from my teeth. The mind that keeps working behind the face, recording the exact shred.

Seamless black, sea risen into a chorus of houses, doors open and wanting.

From out of itself the breakwater, where I left a string of granite against the storm.

Now the hum of sodium lamps along the quay, the flesh of my hands white and foetal.

In this season of spiders who hang by threads, trees are veins against the moon, snow underfoot in misery. The bow I sweep, single flakes of which we name perfection.

(Help me).

HAKAI PASS

Night has laid a heavy tax of stars upon the sky. In hours like these you get up and you speak to the ages, to history, and to the universe.
                    Vladimir Mayakovsky

I do not return from these:

the wave that fell like a door in my camera,
                    caught in its slap of death upon rock it has with gentle
persuasion massaged into West Sand Beach.

And out beyond the lighthouse, Blenheim with its fringe of tree,
rubber-faced sea lions drop from rookeries. The smell of their red
shit where they lay to make it home.

The wolf on the shore of horizontal sun, lifting its water-dripping
face from spiny purple urchins the size of plates.

Memory's habit of forgetting salal, remembering the oriental
pore-sweating heat. Spider Island ripening in fog. This endless
dripping room.

The solid seam of wake pushes steadily from the stern, scuppers
awash with green indifference.

I can accept the sea is marked by the salt that is our dead and the
slow bread of forgiveness, the pink skin of ocean when sun is octopi
stealing from the old Japanese men that dying cedar become.

What is identity but an arm taking hold of itself. I am here and this
is a good.

THE VISITATION OF HAKAI AND

…the dreadful sense of being alone in an empty universe,
the agonies that thrilled through me as if the blood were
running ice-cold in my veins, the disgust with living, the
impossibility of dying.
Hector Berlioz

There is no point giving in to powers beyond your control.

Yanking palomars with my teeth among dolphin leaving their world
like the galloping worms of Dune.

Eagles massing, hunch shouldered in the bent-finger branches,
aboriginal, white-headed gods with no answer but talons.

Slicing cutplug with a skewed knife, brine transforming my hands to
ricotta.

And over my shoulder, in the curl of my head, behind my eyelids,
boxcars of sea coming after me. The wave prevails,

falling forward like a person into the life it doesn't yet know is its own

green promise and end.

And then the true end, sea advancing like the skin of very dead animals.

Full throttle rain hits my face like pieces of wood, the Boston Whaler Outrage now above my eyes, now below.

I remember with affection the three chambered heart banging my hand, wilderness so anonymous it drew the will inside out.

I remember gill plates gagging in too thin air, chinook the length of my leg. And I let go.

Through the night the mist was in the hallways and the generator thrummed the bulging dark. Kurtz that lonely emissary, thoughts festooned and capitulating in relentless jungle.

As though climbing down the tree of knowledge naked apple in hand could pass for a Judeo-Christian act of freedom and compassion.

Then the hook arrives: the maple leaf is a symbol of foreign domination.

HAKAI PASS REVISITED

*Utter darkness is then his light and cat-like he distinctly
sees all objects through a medium which is mere blindness
to common vision.*
                    Herman Melville

Freedom is a hanging thing then the blood jolts my kidneys when I hit.

Quartering Kildaadt Strait into hills of wave beyond my aerial, hand
on the throttle my only connection with earth, or I shall call it that,
the jagged, yawning, steep sea shot with pieces of sun.

Granted there are the fine hours, when I no longer love loneliness,
the fine hours bent like a saxophone player in the pounding rain
under an impossible crooked moon.

Monofilament wraps and cuts my hand and the release of 20-pound
coho, the hooks becoming part of my shoulder, like some friendly,
toothy, hungry alien.

Think of a day as a piece of paper upon which is written the will of
another.

Think of rain so heavy the rest of nature stops to listen and so the
rain is largened.

Think of the tension of rain, holding to itself, so in its coming, glass beads harmless across the Pacific which is its other self.

I am free as long as the rain holds.

Dennis Scissorhands wrapped in electrician's tape to keep nature
from festering, to keep the fish teeth and complaint of invisible
filamentous line from leaving their mark

                                              like the trails of airplanes
bound for Jakarta slice the sky, the dome of blue too far away to be real.
Broken all the same.

THE NEEDLEY TEETH OF SALMON FILL
MY HANDS WITH YELLOW LIQUID

> *Madness, provided it comes as the gift of heaven, is the*
> *channel by which we receive the greatest blessings… madness*
> *comes from God, whereas sober sense is merely human.*
> Socrates

> *Take me… take me.*
> William Peter Blatty

I was not that light but was sent to bear witness of that light.

The NASA gleam of floodlights, fists of salt thrown into yellow buckets, trays of crashing herring.

Pure motiveless muscularity of lightning and beacon that I am with my boat full of gasoline.

The way the littlest insects in a column seek the light between the dying, the decadent hemlock.

Then the wasps on my arms, the blood from many animals, clouds of them wavering above the gutting table.

The time to come is not revealed to me, nor to anyone but the blessed and they are helpless before their gift.

I shall open my hand under the sea and announce my wish to be taken.

The downrigger seizes a piece of watery real estate and zangs its sticky hook off my nail like a bullet off a tin drum.

Salt ridges my unshaven face. My hair like tire tracks, burnt pencils. So free and far away I cannot return.

At the end of it all on the edge the floatplane rises in its own throat into hard things that cannot be seen only touched fatally, this confetti streak, where I sit quietly in my silver jacket with the long wrap-around sleeves.

                    Afternoon moves across the land and sun the wet white lighthouse there on the mustard hill.

FOR DEBORAH WHEREVER
YOU MAY FIND HER

PERHAPS THE FIRST LOVE POEM

No great feat to flick a switch. A lifted finger and the sudden, ambery porch materializes the lesser beings.

In the afterness of sex, I willingly release a sigh. Deborah charts a shirt to a gauzy pattern. Her lips aboriginal, untamable as summer. Pins she plucks from a plush red strawberry.

Maybe Eve didn't like her fruit, a ripe brown fig like a misplaced scrotum in the licheny branches of an apple tree. Maybe the snake

had a hard time convincing her to put it in her mouth, and she, no dummy, had Adam taste a part of himself he never before could reach.

So perhaps it is fruit in my simple hand, perhaps it is pain. I smell sweet seedy genitals across a thin skin of centuries – the thirty-five chemicals it takes to plumpen up an apple!

Or say in my evening chair, about to turn the light like some indulgent immanence, I will recall the delicate toes of elk stepping among the remnant snows indifferent as beauty is to itself;

or, Napoleon in his foolish suede boots retreating from January. The mane of his horse. The way it casually fractured the air.

Every bit as doomed as the soft-winged insects flying resolutely out of nothing. I can do no more than point and say, there goes something dead. Then the smoke lifts from ruined lives.

Deborah has spent her whole life walking toward this orange home. She holds herself among the moving crates, the dried bananas like shrunken heads along the counter. Simple: the meaningless desires with which we fill up our days. And night? Too much of everything.

Which returns me to the pulpy early nectarines, to the question of sex and love, the secret language of our isolated beds of now. The dusky peaks of her pelvic crowns my hand can reach across.

I hold Deb out like a bolt of living cloth, two wrists bound by my right hand, two ankles in my left, and marvel at the rounded female generosity of her flowered blue panties, intuition, where we join in gift.

Which leads me to God. The Bible was written by layers and layers of men who first held up their religion to the scrutiny of themselves, their belief in the very sexual mushroom.

And there is a certain amount of horror, as I grow nimble and fleet of foot, to rephrase the older poet, and shoulder down His long straight road.

And if longing is being stuck, what then ambivalence?

What then if God was one of us?

COMES A SOFT SOFT INSIDE ME I NEVER MEANT TO OFFER UP WHILE TAKING A BITE OF THIGH OR BREAST OR SWAY OF BACK

The black delta
                that bears her mark of passage
                              and ritual cleansing
that is standing in the rain
                    in blue panties
                          once more
I make her Deb and
              water finding the curves
                      of her body where
the sun glances just o

August trees dropping ornaments of rain
                          through the curve
           of sun-splashed hip and defenseless wrist
bent just so
              safe I remind myself
                      rain would not be
        unless it hit the ground.

ANY DECLARATION NO MATTER HOW TENTATIVE IS A TRIP TO SOMEWHERE ELSE

How far in the darkness your roots must travel to send such speaking to the light.
                              Lorna Crozier

Shall I women or uncertainty choose?

Even Nureyev, after hanging longer than any mortal in the sky, had to let his body down at 49.

Christmas day and Deborah of the long black mane comes and vacuums my box of chocolate hedgehogs like some self-appointed goddess of sweets.

The visceral pleasure of licking fingers, disappearing into her, velvet brown.

Thumb on her windpipe, I say, "Imagine the possibility of trust is more than a pile of tubers,

a satin box beautiful under its six warm feet of black. Perhaps you're
alive and no one's coming back because perhaps someone promised,

not some dizzy Adam lounging ho hum on the Sistine dome but some
penis of Donatello told the shifting mourners you were moving on."

On that warm pre-crucifixion day the small conversation of ladybugs
my mind easily mended to grey.

Perfect plastic armour, emissaries bitter as raw potato and slippery,
held their small communion in the spaces in the casement windows.

It's an old old question, the agony of faith and treachery, deformed
metatarsals of the iron butterfly.

For some of the beautiful Florentine men there was male love to
share, HIV.

From the bathroom's nether regions come ladybugs wading the
misty window drinking in the dew.

SHEEPDOGS TRIALS METCHOSIN SUNDAY

White blossoms, then the cherries, now these appetites.
Lynn Davies

...in the collapsing hours when we fall middle-aged together.
Joe Armitage

The lichen-exploded fence owned by someone I know not who
among the Garry Oaks with their tufty little hands of leaves.

Her knee around my neck as casual and intense as an ordinary
flower.

Now her hand is in my arm and we descend thinking of connection,
how some large Hollywood has taken hold,

merging latex and human in some starry explosion.

Oh, yes, of course, there's the spray of sheep, the old green hill the
wind might chase across. But I am thinking

of her bottom as an evening pear and hoping good fortune is more
than a scientific chemical in the scrota.

Civility is a glove we grow into as dust replaces being young, the first
relaxation of skin around the eyes, something to apprehend

where sheep hang whitely down the walls pearls of blood in their
bony nares.

This we call curing meat that is a slow growth of the agents of death
who grant themselves life easier than a bullet

prepares their prey for being devoured; sheep and their tendency to
shoulder together, from fence post to gate to stave to tin whistle.

Oh, and there the other woman with blonding hair I don't think
about anymore. "Dennis, I hardly think

English sheep are bred for their intelligence." Still there is stopping
to be gallant, pulling devil's foot for my own blue Deborah.

Then black bits take the air, Deborah by gorse and asphalt country lane,

waist, coccyx, sacrum I clasp in my hand, the sway back I mount my
pleasure and oh the mops trees make snapped left, right, and I am
convinced

wasps are a constellation of pain from armpit to armpit, throw back
my head and howl I shall come to the meat

at sundown and drink my fill, place the mounds of baking soda until
desire desire me no more.

Sheep dogs, sheep dinner jackets, sheep wolves: ah that woman
dressed in sunglasses draws me against my will.

FOR WOMEN WHO GRAZE THE MELTING FAR

Loyalty to the past is for those who run swords through their heads.
Anon

The hand with all its ageless grace is stupid in winter; the
tadpole pressed turns its stomach from its mouth.
D.C. Reid

I am thinking of the Sistine Chapel and the long slow drip of pigment
to Morrison and Hendrix, Davis and Kobain.

Michelangelo on his back with his palette of nine, six floors above
the floor.

I paint the dipnet swale the fermented shore and bite the skin off my
arm. Snowflakes touch the water like spiders play pianos.

The derelict tractor speaks its absence of people to High Oaks valley,
mud rolled round its wheels. Its fenestrated seat snow with great
patience fills.

There are harrows beneath the flooded fields and beneath them fingerprints to be combed into the dirt.

Auburn hair across a forehead: what is left after longing has left its boot holes in the shore.

Deb's ankle I hold like Clapton, three years since my red-haired child took her tadpoles away.

"Do not be afraid to tell a story with a different ending." In between Deborah's breasts of a girl the black valley that is a lake in its spare time.

How it can pass in and out of existence as though this were easy, as though death changes nothing.

I tell myself I have walked into the open room of the mind, the one where women graze the melting far.

Sun through the screened window and the battering that is insect on the other side of our eyelids soft and futile.

En route to Winnipeg I melt a gun in my hand and from the high cross of an airplane cast lakes across the land.

THINK OF LIFE AS SEVERING CONNECTIONS UNTIL THERE'S NOTHING LEFT TO HOLD US

> *The bird of time has but a little way to fly – and lo! the bird is on the wing.*
>
> Omar Khayyam

> *Touch me I'm so beautiful.*
>
> Indigo Girls

How large a Jesus does it take to throw an airplane into the air so at
its apogee
       a finger pokes through tinfoil and rips a face to pieces?

The aquamarine eggshell of Pan Am 103,
                     captain and crew fallen
from heaven five minutes strapped in their seats, the kiss of
decompression
       having ripped their epaulet uniforms and

underpants from their bodies.

Big Bear waited on the turf in heaps of red and green and yellow blankets.

Eating the tribal dog led to a winter of rickets and wife keening at the
loss of him and dignity,
                          the ebbing out of family in the invisible
country reserved for those who squander their days in any direction
the buffalo might have gone.

The way a vapour on a window will fall into itself and disappear
Deborah turns in the walnut garden. I see the hem of her slip, her
brown thigh,

the plain at the back of her hamstrings to land a thumb,
                          lick a wet runway up her rump, fingers splayed like
toes of pigs.

Out beyond the dunes the shape of young men's breasts
                                          nylon does what it
does in dreams.
            Hold me like a cello in the cold-blooded grip of appetite.
Hold me like a boy.

DEB AT CROSSROADS 46:

Is it getting better or do you feel the same?
Will it make it easier on you now you got someone to blame?
Bono

Memory is amoral, the perfect witness, its desire for itself is
endless and what it takes to be no different.
Anne Michaels/D.C. Reid

I promise what I cannot for you: that the generous might
piece together forgiveness so nothing in the fair decency of
matter is lost.
D.C. Reid

She might close my eyes so no one can see her.

And yes there is strewn seed, nylon on a quadricep.
Sun has conquered the eastern wall, Deborah's toes have climbed the
afternoon long and brown.

"What is bravado but the beginning of regret?" she says and I am a
camera: the way a woman will allow herself to be withdrawn from
panties when she will.

Central Park Lodge, the talcum snap of latex, and gardenia lewd as genitalia. Mrs. Nilsen astride the wheelchair she refuses to vacate. White officiates lift her from toilet and sleep.

"Do I have the currency, dear?" Under lemon windows the questions of a matriarch in padded underpants.

Meanwhile a brown ankle and a sandal strap, a calf I can close my lips around. My face is desired and now the scent of you.

"Do you have a man?" Deborah answers not with language but in her mind, a trick her mother taught well.

Years fell from the white dress spattered with virginity, a colour her father could not see. Her breast the colour of autumn under an addicting moon. "You always liked the men."

And something remains unsaid: that I exist, that I am warm, that I inhabit my days for me,

and all of Deb. For the matriarch inside her skull will rise toward her kingdom at any old golden moment and punch the buttons to the question, "How ever is this debt to be paid?"

Beyond our bed the empty wheelchair. Kindness bangs against me and I am clumsy.

The telephone is ripped from the wall.

DEBORAH THE DIRECTOR WHO STOPS
THE VIOLENCE AGAINST WOMEN

> *Life is a tale told by an idiot full of sound and fury*
> *signifying nothing.*
> > William Shakespeare

> *You asked   for the truth and I   told you.*
> > Sinead O'Connor

How not to want a mother who never wanted you.
And hell? Where old hurts are done and done again.

The 2 x 8 garden plot whacked together from trees some kind logger
separated from their lives. Deborah among the morning gold that
makes me wonder about a person's capacity for pain.

Ma and Pa made a history of draining BC of alcohol in Lazyboy
rockers.

Gin and scotch and beer was the sound of childhood and what she
heard was lips on glass, and cigarettes and Dick van Dyke falling
over furniture.

People sit like they are dead and make themselves more so with a greed that is a silent message to the daughter not spoken to.

Who could object to her sitting in her garden clay on the seat of her sweatpants.

The world sags, the drip of trees, melting of houses, the horizonless horizons without apprehension of the day she faces old with herself because I have been reduced by the bottle without a bottom.

Her focus on the beaten women but not herself, the sty in the eye, the rhomboid that won't, bulimia, the liver that refuses to make the liquor into water, the endless stream of cigarettes and Celaxa.

Dig that trowel and place the shriveled peas and gladiolus, the lettuce, the beets their fat healthy red-spanking bumbs.

Without waywardness we are cattle though they be warm and trusting and good. I go crazy when I look out of other people's eyes.

The rain does not reach her and neither the sun, the image of her body a teenager never grew accustomed to.

ALONE AGAIN WITH THE SCENT
OF YOU ON MY HANDS

I have come more and more to realize that being unwanted is the worst disease that any human being can ever experience.
Mother Teresa

All that is not given is lost.
Indian Proverb

Bats whirl out of the dark, their soft feathery flight thoughts that barely occur

after wind has made the trees into different people. (Your car pulled by to let mine pass and neither did we come to rest, blinded, perhaps, by headlights.)

I have nowhere to go, no Monday, or Tuesday, no daughters, no wife, no woman, no loon with its bush-mad laugh.

As though crossing water that isn't there in all its blackness stands for something else.

Land and pricks of Yarrow Pt. lights in the drip of oars.
I am afraid of myself when I knot my neck and tie the line to the
battery beside the boat and throw my knife ahead of me.

So meat in cheesecloth is the sun I have a weakness for in the eagle
trees.

So my blood turns blue and seeps among the hydrangea nodding
their huge heads.

I say a person dwindles. I say a tear and 10,000 brothers of fog are
the same.

Smoke has taken the northern sky, Crofton accepting bodies of trees
and rendering to chips too small for messages.

FOR DEBORAH WHEREVER YOU MAY FIND HER

Not for us the wedding ring.

The eaves sing in wind that comes from I know not where and goes
to a place much as it came.

Then the emptiness at the heart of the poem, emptiness I turn from
but never to anyone.

The acacia tree and its daggers on which the shrike hangs mice like
used clothes.

We do not break up but apart.

THE EARTH FOR GESTURES
WORDS ARE NOT
ENOUGH

ELEGY FROM A SLUMBER I CAN'T RETRIEVE

Whole sight or all the rest is desolation
John Fowles

While we sleep we sculpt the stories of our days and it is a
kindness that they are hidden
D.C. Reid

Enough of the empty air, what we can see into but not perceive.

Ross Bay cemetery lies under a sky of white fire, the vigilance of June
and lilac.

I watch myself disappear into a distance where I take for granted the
breakwater persists.

Shadows fall long under my feet and I run these 25 miles as though
the walls of fog weren't here and my hands passing through them.

My femur worries its socket that is really my temporal lobe and all
that Byzanteum scientific stuff we believe too much as the second

millennium sails to a close.

I willingly espalier my arms against the white-washed walls of mist and am seduced: the way a

dress renders a woman available to me.

There is the seawall with its haunted forest of rebar. There the shore littered with kelp like the well-oiled bones of black men. And beyond, the sheer lazy roll of green chocolate.

Between my legs my shorts eat holes in my thighs and they are greased by what's inside of them. The blood line slips the quadricep and medial collateral.

Breath rises beyond control, my running shoes at the end of my feet, double-knotted to prevent the Linus Pauling tendency of things to fall apart.

I watch myself disappear, aware that this is not at all possible.

Fog, this fog, is a kind of sleep that moves gently inland until it, too, cannot withstand the sun. Rising with great patience, leonine, the foghorn says to no one in particular,

"I am here, where are you?"

CARMANAH OR THE NATURE OF [1]

The earth for gestures words are not enough.

A native of the Reid family I have no other country than braced between gunwale and fanbelt in which I could be crushed.

Indifferent hills of ocean graze my shoulder, elephantine, tipped with cream.

These miles of ocean lean upon the shore. Mist leaves the trees like old men's hair.

This is wilderness beyond the lighthouse, eye of Carmanah, the last port. The last person comes stumbling from the bush green eyed, different for a time.[2]

As though we could all peer through reality in order to see something more real; the next Galileo or Newton or Einstein, the best of the decimal men, all of us in a kind of family of mutual respect.[3]

Let me, for the moment, luxuriate where I would be: on the undamaged sand.

It is yellow now and I am kneeling among the women, the gorgeous legs of green in the heady scent of morning.

Let me against the barnacles, metal cringing softly, boats against the pilings, creosote in the hand.

Here I be in the high branches with my empty infant face.[4]

[1] Gaya: All the men and all the women would be players now until the world shall free them.[1b]

[2] When his eyes changed colour, L.W. recanted almost everything, yet what we know of it, language continues, a slipshod system for bridging distance.[2b]

[3] J.R.S. is only one who makes the argument that the west is too intelligent, cut off from the rest of itself, a kind of juvenile of the earth. Among the bastards of Voltaire: Loyola and his Jesuits, Richelieu and his Polytechniqe, McNamara with his businesslike approach to the Pentagon, Kissinger in service of the larger ego, his own.

The crowning flower of our wizardry is the arms trade, at $900 billion, the largest component of world trade. Meanwhile, as we make our choices on the stage, the price of one jet fighter would eliminate malaria from the world.[3b]

[4] Adapted from the original by M.B.: a gift of the open eye. All we want is to explore kindness the enormous country where everything is silent. (J.W. in E.M.)[4b]

[1b] There are motions of the earth in which everything is forgiven. (E.M.)

[2b] Even: never losing sight of our left-brained cellular ennui, that a bullet in flight serves no master other than death, we strut the western territory. Among the blue hair lightning, shadows jump away from us.

[3b] Meanwhile, the hidden river of humaness is symbol, ritual and myth.
There are the Hopi who pray for us the sun into the sky each day.
There are the Kogi, licking their sticks, indulging us as younger brothers.
And some of us keep biting the body of Christ for them,
and some of us keep speaking in tongues,
and some of us keep puncturing our bodies with Chinese needles,
and some of us keep spitting mastodons on the walls of caves for
15,000 years.

And among the stars falling into that sky, the killer whale lifts ten tons of black and white in full breech from one element to the next.

[4b] Is this plea? Hope? Compassion?
What we mean, in passing the young of our species into the emptying of ours, we are meant to be loved.   Without reason or end.
The earth for gestures
                    words are not enough.

[1] or the nature of Carmanah *

* Prefatory Acknowledgements: with thanks to Marilyn Bowering, Erin Mouré, John Ralston Saul, J.W. and Ludwig Wittgenstein without whose help this poem's footnotes could not have been written.

WHY WE ENTER EACH OTHER'S LIVES AND HOW
WE FIT TOGETHER IS MORE THAN IS GIVEN US TO
KNOW. AND YET THAT'S WHAT WE WANT, ISN'T
IT? THAT'S WHAT WE WANT TO UNDERSTAND.
Isabel Huggan

Isn't belief necessary all completely wrong familiar sustaining
D.C. Reid

IN THE BEGINNING OF ME IS THE BEGINNING OF EVERYTHING

1959 and the statue memory makes of it

Iwo Jima dusty soldiers pushing a flag for Life

Those summers I stood in the scruffy burnt lot calling grasshoppers

Mortality and Walter Kronkite jungle television of black and white
men slithering down termite mounds and just before carried in a
straight line the 1/2 oz heft of lead through khaki and rib and almost
imperceptible lung and heart and slipped out the back the instant
before surprise set in features 24 muscles of the face

Me in my time capsule which is being an ample green flower didn't
notice so inside my petals

The grandeur of the purple cloud everyone back on their heels in
amazement lifting some human god with powers to let us see
through our arms

And say the purple bones of my purple hand cradled my t-shirt up
and to the left (up and to the left) and I came to honey bee spear out
my arm

Youth a kind of ample green flower

I come a little more among shooting stars inflicting buffalo wallows
with brilliance upon the cracked apart prairie by eons of Fish Creek
tasting the sandstone bluff further than my ears below

The cliff where Peigan drove buffalo saliva crazy tongues and eyes
that went in all directions fleshy veins like rope

The cliff where I raised my arms a conductor of miles of nature
spread out like pristine ruins of greatness to which I am inextricably
bound not against my will at all thinking can I invent a hero

The time I escaped death by fire in the closed room of a forest
cottonwood buds stuck to my summer arm the shrapnel of can
blown so perfectly I found no shred of can on my hands and knees
stamping out strings of fire all over the coulee and the prairie
burning like hair

The sun opens up like fingers on this monument spreading before a
closed-eye face intentional warmth on the cheek skin these memories

My mind the swallows inscribing sky with meaning the odd sense of
perspective happening in those liquid decades

This close

THIS CLOSE A FLUNG ARM IS A GESTURE FUTILE AND GRAND

Only on a plate of Cezanne does the half-eaten apple change not its colour

And so crumpled into being human I left for the continent swirling my Dickensian greatcoat kicking the shingle beach wind blew me into sideways my face my long face

Overman striding to the edge of testosterone this tilt on the Blackpool railing leaning seaward as if a picture caught me just before

And after the pint of bitter and Chinese after the greasy chips in newspaper a fine season with fire jumping out of our bodies a cathedral of candles the lifting of geese from our skin breath in the air angels wringing hands jealous

We have this hole in the mind that fills with theatre observe Canute
in his own crusty century sat in his chair and except for the conviction
of his men might have done otherwise as the treasonous curled his
golden legs

How completely we are forced at the mercy of reliving the past we
may never have lived through and awaken to something no different

Another Globe and Mail flung down among the milk bottles the
oranges the cheese the lovely thumbs-opposable hands
                                                    in a lap

HOW COMPLETELY WE ARE FORCED
AT THE MERCY OF RELIVING

What stories we hold to give the shape a curtain blows into a room
in afternoon

And what to make of small brutalities the freesia smell of Japan for
sale in the kiosk have been cut from their stems

My former monarch has murdered her severed family tactically
separating daughters and father how glorious and regal and years
strutting in crowns of gold only she can see the punishment long
live the king

Nicoleau Ceaucescu comforting his brutal wife to the end the gentle
whump of dust beautiful to the inhumane aesthete an arpeggio of
bullets in a white-washed wall

Comfort not that in Nadezhde's memory she breathed a lifetime's
work to revolt a bit from Stalin Mandelstam the man perished in the
camps humanity in fall appalling

Remembering too I once killed so warmly the bullets skipped from
the river to splash through victims deformed

O fierce and pitiless kingdom of what cannot be undone

O FIERCE SEPTEMBER HERE BRIEFLY BY
THE FOGHORN ON THE POINT

Rumbling left over all morning from the incidental lightning over
the far water and our hair all of our hair standing on the edge on the
shore me

Let me not forget the times I failed to step forward and embrace
someone in my timidity to step forward Robin Charles the others
including myself as yet undead

The score of years cold machinery has taken hunks of my thumb the
blood too solid to do its ritual weeping for itself

This is the violence of fog to confuse without the wonder and safety
there is not a split apart second for holding

We simply must go on courage overcome that which cannot be
overcome turn the page clean the oven and refuse to phrase-make
in approximations

Nothing short of the end of the world as we know it

Now

NOW AND FINALLY THE FESTIVE AMYGDALA

Walnut with the consistency and creaminess of brain between your teeth

And dutifully following my own advice plucking nouns and verbs from red Wernicke and Broca nuclei embroidered with blue left hemisphere and yellow episodic right while pulsing amygdala greens with identity manufacturing history as it is conceived

I tell myself I always see myself looking out my own eyes no more muses for me no fatal attractions

This chore we have of setting and setting out the harbour ice spread in silent complaint against the season from which Christmas has just receded shrieking against the gunwales its anger at our passage easy its brute stupidity sharp as knives upon the hull forcing birth of green water

Out there one time my compass would lead me only east toward
some earlier version of belief and the container ship leapt

I push my face with my thumbs until it's something else the skin of
old men in steam baths the penises of clams the strange and luminous
octopi for sale within their steely jars

2003 and the statue memory keeps shoring up and it inexorable from
our occupied hands all we have say I

ACKNOWLEDGEMENTS

Some of the poems in this book have won awards:

"Eagles," People's Poetry Poem Prize
"Perhaps The First Love Poem," White Water Poetry Contest,
     Silver Medal
"The Hunger," Bliss Carmen Award, Silver Medal

Some of the poems have been published in magazines and on websites:

Prism International, Prism International Website, *Poetry Wales, The Antigonish Review, Capilano Review, Backwater Review, Above Ground Press,* League of Canadian Poets Website, *Prairie Fire, filling station, Prairie Journal, A Time Of Trial Anthology, Hidden Brook Press*

For his support at a critical time in my evolution, Patrick Lane; thank you for telling me the material was good and that my instincts were too. Also Robert Hilles for shaping a shapeless manuscript. Harold Rhenisch for his unending good humour and for his company while driving a gazillion miles, resolutely touring the Golden Triangle. Finally, to the Banff Centre who provided a place to write in a creative circumstance. And, even more finally, to Erin Mouré and Carolyn Forché whose work has meant a great deal to me, for their thumb-printed, coffee-cup-ringed books I have read more times than I remember.